Massive to Micro

Living Things

Look at the **whale**.

Now look at me.

2

Look at the giraffe.

Now look at me.

Share With Me

The giraffe is the tallest mammal on earth. Its neck can be two meters long but it only has seven bones in it!

5

Look at the horse.

Now look at me.

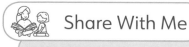

Look at the dog.

Now look at me.

 Share With Me

The largest breed of dog is the Great Dane.
The smallest breed of dog is the Chihuahua.

Look at the **chameleon**.

Now look at me.

 Share With Me

A chameleon's tongue can be as long as its body!

11

Look at the **ladybird**.

Now look at me.

 Share With Me

Tiny they may be but ladybirds can eat up to 5000 aphids in one day!

13

Look at the ant.

Now look at me.

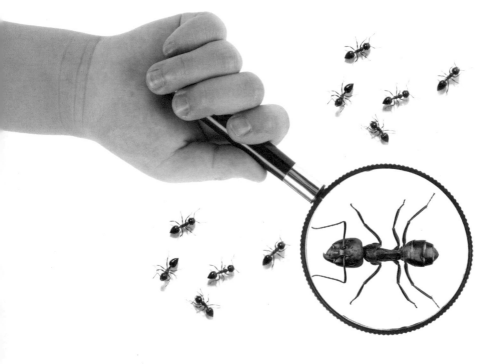

 Share With Me

Ants are tiny - but strong!
They can lift things 20 to 30 times heavier
than they are!

15

chameleon

ladybird

whale